Blue Bird

BY FELIPE COFREROS PH.D.

Order this book online at www.trafford.com
or email orders@trafford.com

Most Trafford titles are also available at major online book retailers.

Print information available on the last page.

ISBN: 978-1-4907-9207-1(s)
       978-1-4907-9208-8(e)

Our mission is to efficiently provide the world's finest, most comprehensive book publishing service, enabling every author to experience success. To find out how to publish your book, your way, and have it available worldwide, visit us online at www.trafford.com

Any people depicted in stock imagery provided by Getty Images are models, and such images are being used for illustrative purposes only.
Certain stock imagery © Getty Images.

Trafford rev. 11/12/2018

www.trafford.com

North America & international
toll-free: 1 888 232 4444 (USA & Canada)
fax: 812 355 4082

BLUE BIRD

Blue Bird sits on a fence.
She watches the sun
rising up in the sky.

Blue Bird flaps her wings and flies up to the sun. "Good morning, sun. You shine brightly early today."

Blue Bird flies down. She passes a tree. "Good morning, tree. Your leaves are green and fresh."

Blue bird looks at the garden. She sees the bees. "Good morning, bees. You visit your flower friends early."

Blue bird flies over the flowers.
"Good morning, flowers. You
look beautiful with your colors
red, yellow and orange."

Blue bird sits on the fence
once again. She looks around.
"It's a beautiful day!"

Exercise 1: Connect the name with the picture.

bird

sun

flower

tree

Exercise 2: Write the picture name in the box.

1. Good morning, [   ] !

2. Good morning, [   ] !

3. Good Morning, [   ] !

4. Good morning, [   ] !

Exercise 3: Color those that the bird has greeted.

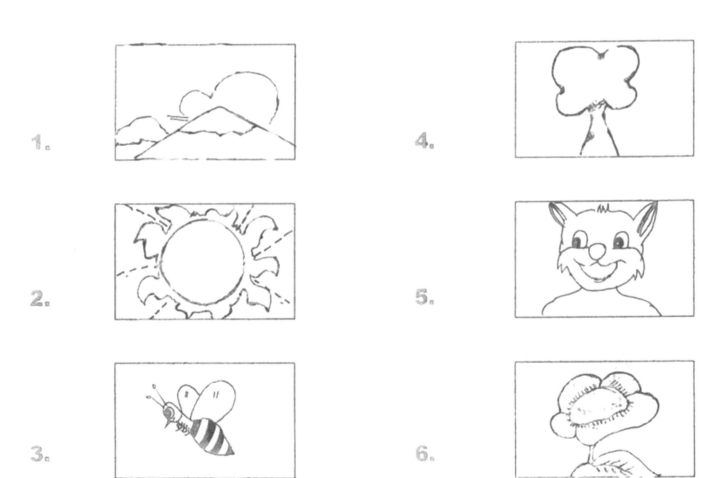

1.

2.

3.

4.

5.

6.

Exercise 4: Connect the lines, then color the flowers as indicated.

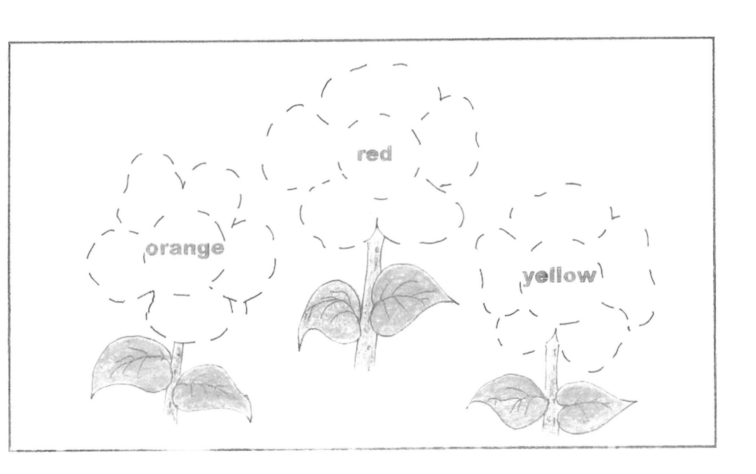

ABOUT THE AUTHOR

Felipe Cofreros Ph.D. spent more than twenty-five years of aggregate experience in teaching Literacy, Adult Education, Pre-school, Elementary, High School, College and the administration of instructional English as a Second Language [ESL] services among Indo-Chinese refugees [Vietnamese, Lao, Khmer and Hmong] in the International Catholic Migration Commission [ICMC], Philippine Refugee Processing Center [PRPC] in Sabang, Morong, Bata-an, Philippines for a decade. Felipe also taught English as a Second Language [ESL] in different countries in Asia and North America. Presently,

Felipe is one of the owners and the Executive Program Director of the International Adult Day Care in Las Vegas, Nevada, USA.

Felipe has authored more than a dozen of Children's Picture Books with comprehension questions for three years old and up geared for use in the preschool classroom; A Handbook of Basic Art, Part 1 [Painting Processes in Playing with Colors, Different Crayon Techniques]; A Handbook of Basic Art, Part 2 [Basic Drawing, Painting and Making Crafts]; Let's Weave [An ancient Hand Art of Interlacing Two groups of Threads]; A Pre-school Math Workbook "Let's Build Our Math Skills Workbook for children ages three years old and up; Effective Ways To Assess English Language Learners [For Intermediate and Advanced Levels]; One Accord - an inspirational book of Bible promises; A Handbook of Writing Activities for Intermediate and Advanced English Language Learners and English Workbook 1, 2 and 3 for the Elementary level.

Felipe graduated as a scholar from the University of San Agustin in Iloilo City, Philippines with a Bachelor of Science in Elementary Education with specialization in Social Studies and Art Education. He also studied Basic Latin, Spanish and Theology courses in the Seminary of St. Augustine in Intramuros, Metropolitan Manila, Philippines. He got his Master's Degree in TESOL and Doctor of Philosophy in Sociology from an on-line University in the USA. Felipe obtained quite a number of certificates in different disciplines such as TESOL Teaching Certificate Course, Lingua Edge, LCC. TESOL Teaching Training Systems West Olympic Blvd., Beverly Hills, California, USA; Managing People for Maximum Performance in John F. Kennedy School of Management, Harvard University, Cambridge, Massachusetts, USA; The Roots of Learning: Society for Effective Affective Learning in Brighton, England, United Kingdom.

Printed in the United States
By Bookmasters